Debt Battle...
Yes, You Can Win!

Arthur A. Arbogast

ISBN: 1499231067

ISBN 13: 9781499231069

Contents

Acknowledgments

I would like to thank my wife, Linda. She is the one that read the manuscript and fixed all my punctuation and spelling mistakes. She is my wife and best friend. Thanks again, sweetheart.

My sister, Becky, has always believed in me and been there for me. I can always count on her.

I want to thank my niece for the pictures in the book. I simply told her the images that I pictured in my mind, and she drew them freehand. Thanks again, Lori!

When it comes to financial mentoring, Frank has taught me so much about investment properties. Thanks so much, Frank.

Eddie is my CPA, and we have become friends over time. We both enjoy getting together and talking about business and investing. He helps keep me focused and motivated.

Most of all I would like to thank God, my Heavenly Father above. I owe everything to Him.

Introduction

When I am asked why I wrote this book, it is a question that has a very deep answer, straight from my heart. This is especially true since I have struggled all my life with dyslexia (a reading disability where written words appear backwards). Why would anyone that has had to work twice as hard with the written word his entire life write a book? As hard as my battle with dyslexia was, my battle with debt was even harder. Dyslexia affects about 10–15 percent of students; debt affects about 65–75 percent of all US families. Debt nearly buried me more than once in my life and has had a devastating effect on the lives of my friends and family. This book is not about how I have learned to "work around" dyslexia; it is about a much tougher battle. I watched people all around me sinking deeper and deeper in debt as I was becoming debt free. I felt compelled to tell someone, to shout, "Hey, wake up and fight back! Don't give in to the habits that have put you in debt and will keep you there!" Becoming debt free is one of the most important things you can do for yourself and your family. I hope this book will inspire you to become, and remain, debt free.

Chapter 1

Starting Out with Less than Zero: Starting Out in Debt

Eight years ago I married a woman that is the love of my life; she is my wife and best friend. I say that for three reasons: first and foremost, it's the truth; second, I will see yet another smile on her face; and third, *Wow! This will score major points for me.* We moved into an apartment within walking distance to my job. The job had good benefits as well as good pay. My wife lost her high-paying job and took on a part-time job that cost more in gas and aggravation than it was worth. The only debts we had were my truck with a payoff of about $5,000, her small student loan of $2,000, and a credit card payoff balance of $5,000. We had over $8,000 in cash, $3,000 in the bank (checking account), and a job with a steady paycheck. This chapter begins the story of how it all went downhill very fast. I think I should, and will, blame myself for what happened next. After all, we live in a push-button, instant-gratification world. Buy it now. Pay for it later! Maybe my life mission statement should have read something like this: spend all your cash immediately, and proudly borrow money if you fall short on cash. This may sound absolutely ridiculous, but this is exactly what I was doing. Spend now; pay later. What a huge mistake that was! This is how it all started snowballing into a big problem, so pay close attention.

I decided my wife needed a new car. Being the car enthusiast that I have always been, I felt it could not be just any car. It had to be a new Mustang! Of course, we would not use that $8,000 cash for a down payment; we were saving that money for fun! Instead we used her paid-for, four-door sedan as a down payment. The car dealership gave us a whopping... (hold on to your hats...drum roll please)...$3,000! After all, we were getting a new Mustang! Also, this new Mustang had to have all the upgraded options: good stereo, upgraded interior, spoilers, even the color we wanted (red). The debt was starting to build, and now we had one truck payment, one car payment, one student loan, one credit card loan—and only one job. We started to use the credit card a lot more than we should have. We were having a good time and having long weekend getaways in our new Mustang. Things were going good! My wife landed a good-paying job, but we were still using the credit card like there was no tomorrow. After about six months of long weekend trips to Florida or the mountains of North Carolina, in our new Mustang, we managed to spend every single dollar of our $8,000 cash reserve (fun money).

Then I decided we needed to have two dirt bikes (off-road motorcycles). Of course, they had to be new ones, plus all of the riding gear, such as helmets, boots, gloves, and all of the cool accessories. Guess how we paid for it? You guessed right! More credit card debt. After about two or three months, I decided we needed two new four-wheelers instead. You know the kind—ATVs (all-terrain vehicles). My wife had fallen from her motorcycle and sprained her wrist. I couldn't even think of her getting hurt worse. We decided ATVs would be safer. So we went to a very large dealership that carried all the major brands. I asked my wife to pick out the brand name and model she liked, and I did the same. We must have looked like two kids in a toy store, running up and down the aisles, looking at and touching all the four-wheelers. Once again, I decided with my appetite and not my common sense. Well, I also needed a trailer to carry the new four-wheelers to the forest, and guess how I paid for all of these new toys? You are wrong. I did not use a credit card. I used a 401(k) loan of $9,000! Wait, it gets better. The truck we had would do the job just fine, but wouldn't a new truck be nice? So after about a year, we traded in the new Mustang. And, yes, we were "upside down." Upside down means the payoff on the car is higher than the value of the car. We got a new truck, and, oh yeah, it had to be a top-of-the-line truck! It was a "Big Red Ram "with an eight-cylinder engine (red again…hmmm). This was yet another one of my poor choices. I was so far upside down financially.

Please keep your seat belt fastened tightly, only one more to go. My wife found a house. As she would say, "a cute little house." It was only about a mile from the apartment we were living in. I could still walk to work, and her new job was less than five miles away. I reluctantly said, "Sure, that sounds OK to me, although I hate to cut grass." On the bright side, we would have a place to keep our new toys in the garage. Also, the house payment was *only* $600 more a month than our apartment rent. *Only* $600 more a month! When you are living financially month to month, paycheck to paycheck, $600 is a lot of money. Looking back, the truly sad part was we could only afford a down payment of $1,500. We almost could not buy it. This might be what the bank would call a bad loan. I don't know—I'm not a banker. One thing I did know: we had so many liabilities.

Webster's New World Dictionary defines liability:
1. **The state of being liable**
2. **Anything for which a person is liable**

Webster's goes on to further define liabilities by introducing the definition of liabilities as an accounting term:
3. *Accounting*: **all the entries on a balance sheet showing the debts of a person or business, as accounts and notes payable, incurred but not paid obligations, and long-term debentures**

The word liabilities can also have a more general definition according to the final definition of this word in *Webster's New World Dictionary*:
4. **Something that works to one's disadvantage**

On the surface I must have looked like a duck on a smooth, ripple-free pond—his head is held perfectly still while little webbed feet moved like rapid-firing pistons underneath the surface. On the surface everything looked calm, but I was in big debt, paddling furiously to keep up. I could feel myself going deeper and deeper into debt. The problem was, I could not stop spending. I don't know if it was instant gratification, the need to have new toys, or possibly the bragging rights of having a new car. Or could it possibly have been me trying to prove to my wife that we could have anything we wanted at any time? Regardless of what the reason was, there was one common denominator. Yes, you guessed right. It was *me*! With my lack of common sense coupled with my poor spending habits, I managed to take a small debt problem and turn it into a big debt problem, all in two years.

Chapter 2

The Wreck and Downsizing

After reading the chapter title, you know this is not going to be good. This is going to leave scars, both physical and mental. It all happened on a beautiful Saturday morning two weeks before closing on the new house. One last good, hard, fast run on the four-wheelers, through the forest on dirt trails and in the mud, before we started to pack boxes for the move into our new house. Yes, you are right. I was riding too fast, throwing caution to the wind, just like I did with my problem of debt. This was a big wreck. My need for speed and lack of caution landed me in the hospital with broken ribs, cuts and bruises everywhere, and (worst of all) a shattered right hand that needed to be rebuilt with screws and wires. (I am right handed.)

The emergency room doctors and nurses and the orthopedic surgeon specializing in hand surgery were all fantastic. Also, my wife was such a blessing. For the next six months, she took me to physical therapy twice a week. Therapy was necessary but very painful with all the screws and wires in my hand. I finally had a full recovery, for which I am truly thankful. By the way, did I mention the bills did not stop? Actually, they got worse. Yes, we had medical insurance, but we still had a lot of extra medical and therapy bills that were not covered in our insurance plan. Also, I was drawing short-term disability pay, which was only 65 percent of my full pay. Again, I am truly grateful we had that income. It could have been so much worse if I had worked for an employer that did not offer such good benefits. Still, when it came to money, things were not looking good. Now instead of living month to month, we were living week to week. We started to receive those annoying phone calls from our creditors. Twice, our phone got shut off due to lack of funds, and once, our electricity got shut off. Then we had to start paying late fees because we did not have the money to pay on time. Since we had to start paying late fees, this made an already big problem bigger, (bottom line—even less money). This was a serious low point in my life financially. Special thanks go to my wife. Because of the strong bond we have together, we managed to keep our heads above water while swimming in debt. Finally, after months of agonizing therapy and annoying phone calls from creditors, I was released to go back to work with no physical restrictions.

Do you remember when the housing market tanked in 2008, and the economy started its down turn? I sure do! I had only been back to work for three months when my manager informed me that due to the economy and lean manufacturing, there were to be cutbacks. He informed me that I still had a job, but he could not tell me what shift or what department, and most likely it was to be at less pay. I didn't know if I was sad or mad. After over thirty years of hard work and dedication at the same company, surely this could not be happening to me! But it was!

After a weekend of thinking about it, my wife and I decided I needed to walk away from this company. Not only would I lose good pay with good benefits, but I would also lose over thirty years of friendships. This meant hundreds of people I would never see again. Looking back, I think that was the hardest part. I would miss all of those good people I worked with. I felt as if I were being thrown out like a pair of worn-out shoes. My financial planning was in the toilet, and my job soon found its way there also. The question is, "Whose hand was on the flush lever?" Was it the company? Was it the economy (our government)? Or was it my own hand? I was desperately looking for someone to blame; I should have been looking for a new plan.

What I did next may not have been the best thing to do, but I did it anyway. I decided to quit or, shall I say, *retire early*. Also, I decided to start receiving my early retirement pay at the age of fifty-five instead of waiting until age sixty-two. The problem was that the amount of money would only be 65 percent of full retirement pay due to a reduction of 5 percent per year for receiving this money before the age of sixty-two. Also, I was only fifty-two at the time, so I had to wait three years until I could start receiving my reduced retirement pay. I reasoned that in three years, reduced retirement pay would be better than no pay.

Looking back, it was absolutely ridiculous to think that the company was the problem. The problem was me and my poor financial planning. I'm the one that caused the debt, I'm the one that did not have an emergency fund, and I am also the one that did not have a plan for my retirement. There was no one to blame except myself. Jobs are temporary—they come and go—but your financial future is yours for the rest of your life, so you need to start taking financial control now! It's hard to believe I did not realize this until I was in my fifties. In my twenties my attitudes and actions reflected the intent to live for today and not worry about tomorrow. Buy it now—pay for it later! I remember older and wiser people who cared about me would always want to talk to me about my financial future. I would politely ignore them. I was too busy playing sports and racing cars or motorcycles to take the time to learn finances. How the tide has changed; now I seek out mentors. If only I could turn the clock back, I would've started taking financial control when I was in my early twenties. The good news is that it is never too late to start taking control of your finances. I suppose it's like a good diet and exercise plan: it's better to start late than to not start at all.

A few days ago, while I was working out at a fitness center, I heard a commercial on TV, or maybe I should say I could not help but hear the commercial. It was blaring in my ear, and I felt as if my head would implode. It was a commercial about a car dealership. The guy on TV said that he had just lost his job, but luckily he found another job, so he went out and bought a new car from this particular car dealership. It's sad to think that there are so many people who feel that if they get a new job, they need a new car. Or if they get a pay raise, they need a new car. Or something even more ridiculous, like a car lease, which is nothing more than a big rental with four wheels. This is very hard for me to say and even harder for me to do because deep down inside I am still a huge car enthusiast. Just remember, if you have a big car payment and then lose your job, have an illness, or have a serious accident like I did, you may lose that new car. Luckily, we did not lose our car. Like I said before, it could have been so much worse.

Chapter 3

No One to Blame
Except Myself

So there I was—without a job, after over thirty years with the same company, and swimming in debt. We were blessed that my wife still had a good-paying job. OK, let's look and see how much of a debt problem I managed to get myself into. Please remember, debt knows no difference between high-income earners and low-income earners. Debt is like a blood sucking leech; it only feeds on bad spending habits. Believe me; I had plenty of bad spending habits.

All of my life I have believed in *buy it now, have it now—pay for it later*. Do you remember earlier when I said the economy took a downturn and the housing market tanked? We were upside down on the house to the tune of about $45,000. We owed over $140,000 on a house we would be lucky to sell for $95,000. Our credit card debt was $20,000, our new truck payoff was $14,000, our 401(k) loan was $9,000, and our other truck payoff was $2,000. There were also a few leftover medical bills from the accident. With our $140,000 mortgage, this added up to around $190,000 in debt. With only one job, that was a little scary. Luckily, the student loan finally got paid off. Also, we still had monthly bills such as auto insurance, utilities...oh, and let's not forget food. I remember those days when I would pay my bills according to the due date on the bills. You know you are in financial trouble when you sit down to write out your bills and you use your checking account balance and the calendar at the same time. All the while, you are asking yourself, "When is the bill due? When do I get paid again?" Our entertainment money still existed—we made sure of that—but it was a very limited amount.

Let me get off track a bit here with a few examples of what we did when we were short on entertainment money. We would take a lunch and our bicycles to a county or state park for a picnic and ride. You can normally get into the parks for about five to ten dollars and enjoy exercise and fresh air for the day. What a great deal! We would see people there having fun throwing Frisbees, playing guitars, and rollerblading. Going to a local car show can be great fun. They're almost always free, and if they do charge money at all, it's very little. If you live close to the beach or a lake, you can go there. It's fairly inexpensive. You can usually find a local establishment there that overlooks the water, and have a cheeseburger. There's something magical about a cheeseburger at the beach. That's only three examples of what we did. You do not need to spend a lot of money to have a lot of fun. Also, it is quite possible you will have more fun after you realize you are spending less money! Since I have gotten off track a bit, I'm also going to jump ahead a bit. Becoming debt free can hugely increase your quality of life. After you are debt free, do not be surprised if you feel as if you received a huge pay increase. You may even feel like you doubled your income. You will be amazed at how much money you actually have once you are living debt free.

So there I was, fifty-two years old with no job and high debt accompanied by very high stress due to high debt. My anxiety level was so high that it was off the charts.

Webster's New World Dictionary defines **debt**:
1. **Something owed by one person to another or others**
2. **An obligation or liability to pay or return something**
3. **The condition of owing (to be in debt)**

Special thanks to a great and understanding wife who is younger than I. She is only fifty. (Ha ha!) I decided I needed another job—very soon. The first job I applied for, I got. The pay was OK. The problem was it was a second-shift position. That shift actually became a good thing. I will explain that later. New job, same old bills! Deep down I knew what the problem was. It wasn't the money I was making; it was the money I was throwing away. Spending, spending, and more spending! The problem was me! Let me repeat that—the problem was me! I was the person that caused this debt problem, so I was the only person that could fix this debt problem.

If you are reading this book, there is a strong possibility you have debt problems. Maybe it's not to the extent I had, or possibly it could be much worse than I had. The debt may be solely your problem, or it may be the result of a joint effort between you and your spouse. Regardless of whether it was you or your spouse, or both, that caused the problem, debt is a bad thing. In my opinion it only seems to get worse as time goes on.

It was not necessary for me to become an expert in the study of stress to know how debt added stress to my life. I knew my stress was compounding day by day. I'm sure people around me could sense my high anxiety due to my big debt and lack of money. I think I was at maximum stress level. This high stress was quite possibly the culminating point. This is what it took for me to make a change. Looking back, it's hard to believe I could not have a new car without having a car payment to accompany it. For thirty years I had been on a vicious cycle of debt. This was causing a downward spiral of my mental well-being. The older I was getting, the more debt I was acquiring. Financially I was not progressing: I was regressing. My problem with debt was not hard to fix. It only took time and determination. I did it, and I'm definitely not a financial genius. All my life money has come in one hand and gone out the other. I needed to make a change. I knew what the problem was. Now, what could I do about it? And how could I change it?

Chapter 4

That's It! No More!

At the time I did not know what to do. I just knew something had to be done, and it had to start with me. Sure it would be easy to blame someone or something else. You know—the housing market, jobs, economy, politics, and the list goes on and on. One thing I did not need to do was to shift blame. In actuality I was still the problem. I got myself buried in debt, and only I could get myself out. I had one thing going for me...tenacity! I think I have had that all my life. When I was younger, whether I was playing sports, riding wild horses in rodeos, racing cars, racing motorcycles, or learning to fly airplanes, deep down inside I have always had a strong determination to complete whatever I set out to do.

I think everyone has the potential for personal motivation, drive, and determination, but when it comes to debt, we all say the same thing: "I will catch up on that bill next month," or

"Maybe I will do a little more overtime?" Does any of this sound familiar? The problem is that next month is almost here, and more overtime money will not fix your problem. Your spending habits will. I believe shopping and spending can become habit forming. Let me repeat that...**I believe shopping and spending can become habit forming!**

I read a 2011 statistic that said on Black Friday weekend (one of the biggest shopping weekends in the United States), there were 152 million shoppers, and sales totaled $52 billion. Cyber Monday sales are also growing rapidly. I know a woman who is so obsessed with shopping that she uses her vacation days from work to go shopping. She told me she has over one hundred pairs of shoes in her closet, and some of them she has never worn. One day I asked her if she had plans for Thanksgiving, which was only about a week away. She informed me she had big plans for the day after Thanksgiving...Black Friday! On this huge shopping day, she was going to buy a new "top-of-the-line" flat-screen TV. Puzzled, I asked if her TV was broken. She said, "No, I have three, but after Thanksgiving there is one going on sale, and it's a great deal that I can't pass up." This is one example of someone I know that is obsessed with shopping and spending. Even more worrisome, she tells me she uses her credit card because she has no money. *She is using her credit card to supplement her money shortage*!

I hear it all the time: "I would have more money if it were not for this motorcycle payment," or "I sure wish my car insurance, car payments, and taxes were cheaper on my new exotic sports car," or "I deserve these vacations; I work hard!" I know someone who saves a lot of money throughout the year so he and his family can take a two-week vacation to a faraway destination. For two weeks he and his family live well beyond their means and spend money as if there is an endless supply of it. After two weeks of fun, it's back to work for fifty weeks, saving money so he and his family can do it all again next year. There is nothing wrong with taking vacations, but just think about how much money he would have if he used some of that money for investing. If he can save that much money for a vacation, he should also be able to save some money to invest for his future. Maybe he could rethink his priorities. That's what I had to do. I had to make a choice. I could remain in debt for the rest of my life by spending beyond my income, I could work long hours for fifty weeks and then enjoy two weeks of living like a king(similar to what my friend is doing), or I could start now investing in my future. That way my money could do some or all of the work for me in the future. I did not want to load this book down with a lot of boring line charts or pie charts, but here are a few statistics I feel you really need to see. As you read these statistics, please do not just speed-read through the numbers. Look at the numbers, and think about what they really say about our spending habits.

As I was looking at statistics on debt, I received a meeting cancellation, so I decided to go for a long walk to get some exercise and fresh air. I saw something that made me think about myself just a few short years ago. I saw someone driving a new truck pulling two new jet skis. I thought to myself that must be what I looked like when I had a new truck and two new four-wheelers. I wondered whether he was in debt as bad as I was, and if so what a sad and helpless feeling that was.

American Family Financial Status	Data
Average American family savings account	$3,800
Percent of working Americans who are not saving for retirement	40%
Percent of American families who have no savings at all	25%
Average American household debt	$117,951
Percent of American workers who postponed their retirement age this year	24%
Percent surveyed who are very confident about having enough money for retirement	18%
Percent of American adults who have an emergency fund to fall back on	38%
Source: Federal Reserve, US Census Bureau, Internal Revenue Service Date Verified: 7-26-2012	

So no more excuses. I've heard them all. As a matter of fact, I think I've used them all. I realized I was in a fight, a debt battle. A battle I was not going to lose. In my golden years, I was not planning on eating dog food or pushing a discarded grocery cart, picking up cans beside the highway. I was definitely not counting on looking for help from the government in the form of social security. I don't know if that money will be there when I reach my golden years. After all, you know what kind of financial savvy the government has. They're going into debt faster than I did. Wow! Now that's a scary thought!

So for the next two months, all I did was pay bills, observe my financial habits and the financial habits of those around me, and take a lot of mental notes. It may have appeared that I was doing nothing, but it is all part of the way I prefer to process things and develop plans. For example, if I decide to start jogging, I like to wear my jogging shoes for one or two days before I start running. If there is an important task that needs to be taken care of, I need to think about it for a few days and develop a plan before I start to work on it. I feel it is wiser to plan first and react second. That's just me! The big question was, "Where was the money going?"

My wife and I decided to cut back on our spending, although we still went out for dinner from time to time and kept our date nights. I think that is very important and healthy for a marriage. So even after the spending cutbacks, it was still month to month, week to week, paycheck to paycheck, and bill after bill. There was no end to those persistent monthly bills and an occasional late fee. Those late fees bothered me the most. Late fees! I paid more money out each month because I didn't have the money to pay on time. I understand why I paid more, but it didn't change the fact that I didn't like it. That just bothered me!

Doing nothing toward debt reduction for two months while struggling to make all those credit card and car payments may not have seemed like the smartest thing to do, but I think that was my way of preparing for this debt battle. I needed to develop a plan of attack. Until now I had been losing this debt battle all my life. Things were about to change. I was going on the offense, and I was going to start doing the attacking. This was my personal battle against debt. This was a battle I was not going to lose! I needed to empower myself and take charge of my own finances. I needed to take full responsibility for my financial future. I needed to take a long hard look at my life's values. I needed to become more proactive.

> *Maybe I should not be saying I, I, I and should be saying He, He, He because God is leading my wife and me down the path we both need to be following, and debt is not part of that plan.*

Being debt free was much more important than continuing to have meaningless material things. This is the conclusion I came to and I resolved to change. What about you? Is reading these words hitting home? Are you ready to change and make positive decisions that will affect your future?

Fortunately, I'm blessed to have a Heavenly Father above as well as a wonderful wife that stands beside me (not in front of me and not behind me, but beside me). She knew with my integrity, focus, and strong determination, I would be able to get us out of debt. Going into debt is easy. Coming out of debt is not hard—it just takes time, determination, and rethinking your priorities.

And let me tell you, it feels great when you see that debt disappearing! After you pay all those credit cards off and get that car paid for, it feels like a huge weight has been lifted off your shoulders. Hopefully your debt reduction will help reduce your stress levels, and possibly you may get along with people better. For me debt reduction has helped with my physical and mental well-being. It has helped me become less abrasive with people. I have become happier, healthier, and wiser because of this debt reduction journey and it feels great. Give it a try.

If I may make a suggestion, spend the next two or three months taking notes and writing down everything to do with your money, regardless of how insignificant you think it is. List all money coming out of your pocket whether you use cash, debit card, or credit card. Include the wasteful spending trips to your favorite clothing store, the candy bar out of a snack machine, plus the bag of chips and soda at the convenience store. This all adds up very quickly. After two or three months, you will see how much wasteful spending you are actually doing. It's possible you may be wasting one-fourth or more of your pay for junk you do not need. This is the same as if you take one-fourth of your money, every time you get paid, and throw it in the trash can. Poor spending habits got me in trouble with debt, and it's probably the same for you. Be honest with yourself. Is it your poor spending habits? Write everything down. It will be a great snapshot of your actual monthly expenses as well as monthly waste.

Chapter 5

Let's Get Started

Do you remember in an earlier chapter I said I would explain later how second shift turned out to be a good thing? Well, now is later. Getting home at a late hour after working the night shift seemed to be a perfect time to start studying finances, debt, and money in general. I think a person can become very good at something he or she wishes to do. So I decided I needed to be good at finances and debt reduction. When I got home from work, it was late at night, and my wife was asleep so she could wake up at five the next morning for her job. I decided I would use my evenings after work to study. Besides, other than watching late-night TV alone, I didn't have anything else to do.

My wife and I do not watch much TV, very little as a matter of fact. We both think it's a big waste of time. I recently heard a commercial on the radio make the statement that if you used their TV service, you could record and save a ridiculously high amount of hours of TV programs—in addition to the TV programs you are already watching. Don't you think a little extra time spent on finances and personal development would be more beneficial? In my opinion most of the TV programs I've seen are very rude or extremely stupid. Not to mention the continuous bombardment of commercials, always trying to get you to buy things you probably don't need. Oh yeah...how do you think you got in debt to begin with? Probably by buying things you didn't need. When you limit TV watching and begin your own debt battle, you start to look at TV commercials with a much more objective view. Why do otherwise intelligent adults need to hear a child in a car seat tell them what kind of car they should be driving? Or do we as bill-paying heads of households really want to hear a teenage girl insinuate we are not as smart as she is because we do not have the same type of phone plan she has?

Yesterday morning I turned on the TV (which is a rarity in itself). The TV had been on less than five minutes when the barrage of commercials started—fourteen to be exact. Yes, I counted them, and two of the commercials were dramatic teasers about the weather and the depressing stories coming up on the local evening news. I grabbed the remote, turned off the TV, and said aloud what a big waste of time that was!

OK, no more about TV. Sorry about that little swerve in the road; now back to the story. My wife was offered a job promotion. For about a week, we discussed the positive points as well as the negative points. The good news was that it was a great career move into a job she still enjoys, plus a pay increase. The bad news was she would be training out of town for six months. Although, I must say, the company she works for was more than generous. In addition to the pay increase, they also paid for airfare every thirty days so she could fly back home or I could fly to go see her, whichever worked best for our schedules. So she accepted the job offer. We decided that a small sacrifice then would pay huge dividends in the future. Since she was gone on an out-of-town work assignment, I was coming home after work to an empty, lonely house, with nothing to do except play my guitar poorly or continue to study finance. Well, this book is not about playing guitar poorly! So I continued studying finance with even more intensity and drive than ever before. I think I was becoming obsessed with it.

The first thing I needed to do was get a handle on those late fees. They can add up quickly. I was getting about two or three late fees a month. Make it a priority to stop paying late fees as soon as possible. If you owe the money, you pay the money, but there is no reason to pay more than you owe! Also, this sets the stage for the debt battle. If you're preparing for a debt battle, late fees can make you feel like you've lost the battle before you have even started. Remember, debt is your enemy! I was paying close to twenty dollars a month in late fees. That's ridiculous! Also, if you do not have the money to get your bills current, you may want to think about selling something you don't need, like maybe that extra set of golf clubs you are not using. Maybe someone where you work has offered you money for those good tennis rackets in the back of the closet that you can't remember the last time you used. Or what about that old boat in your backyard that has not moved in five years, that you are still paying insurance and taxes on? OK, think about this for a minute. You have not used the boat in five years, and chances are you will not use it this year. Sell the boat, get the money, and think of how much money you saved by not paying taxes or insurance on something you're not going to use.

In a small two-mile radius where I live, I can point out four boats and three campers that have not moved in over five years. Remember, you need to rethink your priorities. In this stage of your life, what is more important to you—keeping those old golf clubs or the boat you are not using, while you remain in debt, or selling them as a start to becoming debt free? Debt is your fault, and only you can fix it! Believe me, it is not hard to fix.

Chapter 6

The Budget

If you're like me, the word *budget* frightens you. As a child that word meant I was not going to get a new basketball because it was not in the "budget." I had to continue to play with the old ball that would lose air after about fifteen minutes. I would just improvise and take the air pump to the basketball court. My parents did the best they could, and I'm very thankful for what I did have. Many years later, as an adult, my view of a budget remained skewed. As an employee, I remember going to those yearly company meetings with about six or seven of the upper management team on stage ready with prepared speeches. Each one would get about ten to fifteen minutes to talk about his or her area of expertise regarding all the different departments, and the company in general, while armed with pie charts flashing by at break-neck speeds and laser pointers dancing off the walls like a rock concert. The last one behind the podium would begin something like this: "Due to poor sales..." or something equally as frightening about the economy. Then he or she would talk about tightening the budget. I would hold my breath for a moment because I knew that meant no pay raise, or if so it would be a smaller percentage rate than the inflation percentage rate. Also, there was that word *budget* again.

My thoughts about a budget and budgeting have changed dramatically. You should try to think of it as a great tool, a tool that will help you achieve your financial goals. When you sit down to start working on your new budget, hopefully your spouse is onboard with it. This will make it so much easier. Also, be very honest. The first budget you put together may make you realize you have more money than you thought; you just didn't know where the money went (poor spending habits). This will be the start of your debt reduction.

When I said you *have* more money than you thought, maybe I should have said you *had* more money than you thought (poor spending habits). How about this for an example? On your way to work, you spend about two dollars for a cup of coffee. That adds up to forty dollars a month (if you are working five days a week). When you get to work, you buy another cup of coffee and a little snack that costs a total of about three dollars. That is about sixty dollars a month. The total of these three small items is one hundred dollars a month for two cups of coffee and a snack. I'm not saying not to drink coffee. All I'm saying is why not have a cup of coffee and a piece of toast or an apple at the house before you leave for work? This is just one example of how you can revise spending habits. You will find the ones that work best for you.

When you and your spouse sit down to work on the budget, please be very open and honest about your spending habits. Do not say you spend seventy-five dollars for a round of golf when you know it is actually one hundred dollars after you count in food and lost golf balls. Wait, that's how much you spend on coffee and snacks per month! Hey, a good budget does not stop you from having fun. It is only a great tool to help you know where the money is going. How do you know how much money you have if you do not know how much money you have spent? There is a large percentage of couples who hide money from their spouses, who also have separate bank accounts, and do not tell their spouses how much money they have in that account. How can you have a good budget if you're not honest about the money? If you have a good, strong marriage, you need to also have a good, strong budget. In my opinion that will only help a marriage. Most statistics I have seen on marriage problems show that money is almost always toward the top of the list of things that couples argue about. Without arguing, without blaming, and without finger-pointing, discuss the budget, total money, total expenses, and total money waste (poor spending habits). My wife and I have separate checking accounts, but it is for our convenience only. We both know how much money is in all of the different accounts.

I know someone that has, and brags about having, seven pairs of designer sport sneakers and cannot afford a forty-dollar ticket for a local sporting event. If he only had a budget! I overheard two women talking about shopping, and one said to the other, "That's expensive. That's a car payment!" Since when is a car payment a standard to measure money? To this day I am still amazed and on the verge of being speechless when I hear that phrase, "That's expensive. That's a car payment."

However, on the flip side, I have seen children with better spending habits than some adults. Here's a perfect example. About two weeks ago, I was in the checkout line at a grocery store. There was a woman in front of me putting her food on the conveyor belt. She had two young children, a daughter about four years of age and a son that looked about five or six. As the cashier was scanning the woman's food, the cashier came across a small toy. The woman politely asked the cashier to check the price of the toy. The cashier said it cost $1.80.

The woman looked at her son and said, "It is one dollar and eighty cents. Do you still want it?"

He thought for about three or four seconds then said, "No."

I was very impressed with this woman. She is teaching her children not to be impulsive buyers. I assumed that money would be coming out of her son's own pocket. A young child of that age felt that little toy was not worth $1.80. Good for him and that family.

Surely you know this guy. He always shows up, whether you work at a small company, a large corporation, or on a jobsite. This is the guy that scrapes loose change off the floorboard of his car for gas money and has holes in the bottom of his shoes but somehow manages to get a new motorcycle financed. He is also the first one to volunteer to work overtime to make the motorcycle payments. Tomorrow when you go to work, look around and you will spot him, if you don't already know who it is. Hopefully it is not you. I must confess it was me when I was in my twenties.

As you're reading this book, I hope you don't get the impression that my wife and I do not buy things. We buy what we need when we need it. We are just much wiser than we used to be about our spending. For example, not long ago I needed a new suit jacket. We went to a well-known retail store, and in about ten minutes we found a brand-name suit jacket that fit perfectly. It was exactly what I was looking for, and the best part was that this jacket was discounted 70 percent! I only had to pay $72 for a $240 suit jacket. It seems the less concerned I am about shopping the better the deals are. If I need something, I go in the store and buy it and then leave. I do not treat shopping as a form of entertainment.

Special thanks to my wife and her computer skills. We now have a fantastic budget on the computer. All we do is plug in the numbers. If you or your spouse cannot create your own, there are several reputable companies that sell books on budgets or software that contains templates for budgets. Ask at your local bookstore. The staff can be very helpful and point you in the direction where these books are located. My first budget was put together with paper and pencil. It looked more like a list of people we owed money to and not much like a budget, but it worked just fine. If it's a simple, basic budget, that's OK. A simple budget is better than no budget. A simple budget will help you get started in the right direction for your debt reduction plan. It can help reduce your stress level by taking the mystery out of where your money is going. You can develop a more detailed, complex budget later. I must admit that I have gone back to the "old-school" method of a pencil and a paper budget book. That just seems to work best for me. (I don't have to wait for my computer to start up every time I want to record items in the budget!) Whatever works best for you is what you should go with. Do not think you need to be "tech savvy" to be debt free. You should be able to find the paper-type budget books online or in an office-supply store. Remember, it's your budget. You choose and use whatever works best for you. Do not be surprised if you have to change some of your expense numbers from time to time. It may take a few months to get your expense numbers set. Also, as you pay off bills, your monthly expenses will change again, so do not be alarmed. The more you see your debt reduce, the more enthusiasm you will have for keeping a budget. Just keep modifying and working the budget, and you will see your financial transformation happening right in front of you!

Chapter 7

Emergency Stash

This next item is a milestone that may sound difficult at first, but it is relatively easy, much easier than I first thought. I needed to have an emergency fund of cash, and I do mean emergency only. Somewhere between $500 and $2,000 are the numbers I have seen in many financial and self-improvement books. I decided that $1,000 seemed to be an easy number to remember as well as an obtainable amount to save. There are many ways to come up with the money. Do you remember the idea about possibly selling something you do not need, like that extra set of golf clubs or that old boat? What about those tax refund checks that somehow disappear every year? Maybe where you work you get those quarterly or yearly bonuses? (Don't laugh—some companies still do that.) Also think about how much money you are saving per month by not stopping for coffee on your way to work. You can do this. I know you can. Even if it takes three months, four months, or a lot longer than that, stick to it. If you are able to save and put aside your emergency stash money in only two months, that's even better. If it takes five or six months, that's OK, just stick to it. This is your first hurdle. Remember, stop buying junk you do not need, and put that money in with the emergency cash fund. When I say emergency, I do mean emergencies only.

I remember many years ago I had to evacuate due to a very large approaching hurricane. On the day of evacuation, all the stores, gas stations, and banks were closed. I stopped at the ATM machine on my way out of town to get some cash. It would not give out money, and it kept my one and only debit card. **I had no money or ATM debit card**! If only I would have had an emergency stash, my evacuation out of town could have been so much easier. Luckily, I was with a group of friends, and they helped me out. If you have very little money, fixing or replacing a flat tire that prevents you from going to work may be an emergency. A better TV to watch a ball game is not an emergency. Think about your priorities, about what is important, and about what is not important.

Let me ask you a question: do you know this guy? He is quite possibly a good friend of yours who always pays you back but always seems to need to borrow twenty dollars from you the day before payday, almost every month. That's what I did for years. I definitely did not have an emergency stash. As I'm saying these things, please remember I have been there and know the feeling of paycheck-to-paycheck living.

When you are living from paycheck to paycheck, things always seem to be breaking, like the radiator in your car, the water heater in your house, or even the toilet. The list goes on and on. Please remember that the money in your emergency stash is for emergencies only. Also, think about this very important point. This will make you feel good and may help with your motivation. After you become debt free, even these things that I just mentioned are not emergencies anymore; they are merely minor inconveniences or small speed bumps on this road of life. You will not worry so much if an item in your house needs replacing or if your car needs maintenance. You will have already budgeted money for those things. Until then, remember that a new stereo for the car, a new set of golf clubs, a vacation getaway, birthday gifts, or Christmas gifts are not emergencies. I hate to be brutally honest, but working on your budget and getting your finances in order should be your priority. Gifts and celebration should be modest and should be within your budget. Stay the course in your commitment to financial freedom. Those people that really matter and really love you don't care about the price of the gift—only about the thoughtfulness of you remembering them.

Speaking of Christmas and gifts...let me tell you what my wife and I like to do about gift exchanges between the two of us. Keep in mind that since we have reduced our debt, we could afford to spend more money, but we choose not to. This is a lot of fun. Maybe you should try it yourself and not go into debt over Christmas gifts. My wife and I think that Christmas is a very spiritual time of the year. It goes much deeper than just buying gifts for people, but we still buy thoughtful, inexpensive gifts for family. We **really** get into the spirit of shopping for each other though. The way we do it is different. We do not use credit cards. All year long we save our change in a bucket. A lot of grocery stores have the machines that you pour change into. It spits out a receipt that you can cash in. The machine charges about 6–8 percent, but that's OK. We have fun with it. We both always guess how much money it is and see who is the closest. It usually adds up to about $300 or $400. It's fun to walk out of a store with more money in your pocket than you walked in with! This only happens once a year. The important thing is that you are learning to save money throughout the year, and you will be able to see how much loose change will add up to in one year's time. You are also learning how to manage your money, even if it's only loose change. It's the good habit you are starting that counts.

Now that we have our Christmas cash, we have a scavenger hunt. We sit down ahead of time and write down five things we both would like. We do not get specific. Instead, they are items like a CD, a funny T-shirt, a book, a Christmas ornament, something from a toy store, and so on. We both have the same list, and we have a one-hundred-dollar limit to buy all five items that we think the other person would like to have. We need to get as close to one hundred dollars as we can without going over. It's a lot of fun, and we do not go into debt doing it. Give it a try. You may find yourself having fun. Every year we change the list. One year we had a list that looked like this: something nautical, something automotive, something you would find at the beach, something historical, and something from the grocery store. An example of something you would find at the beach? Use your imagination. Be creative— beach chair, beach blanket, seashells, flip flops, sunglasses, suntan lotion—because there are lots of things to choose from! Change up the list, and have some fun on less money. Also, by using cash instead of a credit card, I think you pay closer attention to your spending. If you have kids, you may need to spend that money on them. It's your money. Do what is best for you and your family.

Have you ever noticed that retail stores encourage you to use their in-store credit card instead of your bank credit card or cash? Is it so retail stores can save money by reducing the number of employees they need, or is it so you will spend more by using a credit card? You be the judge of that. Also, if a retail store "gives" you a discount when you use their in-store credit card, it is because if you do not pay your balance completely each month, you will be charged an interest rate that most likely will far exceed any savings from the discount. The stores are very wisely counting on the fact that most people do not pay their credit card balance each month. You can be wise, too.

Remember, an emergency fund is for emergencies only. Christmas is not an emergency. Get creative in your expression of love for your friends and family. I believe a great side effect of your debt battle could be that your family will grow closer, get more true enjoyment out of life, and become less enslaved to the chase for materialistic stuff. Save your emergency stash for the true emergencies in your life.

Chapter 8

Payoff Is the Fun Part

This is where it gets interesting and fun at the same time. Before I start, remember I am not a financial expert. I'm not saying my way is right or it's wrong. I'm simply saying this is the way I did it. I'm sure a financial expert can argue this point with a lot of numbers and percentage points, but my battle was not with a financial expert. My battle was with my own debt. I am winning decisively, although I still have a mortgage. I will explain that part later. The hardest part of this battle is already over—changing your poor spending habits and establishing a good budget. A few days ago, I saw a commercial on TV or heard it on the radio. I don't remember because I don't pay close attention to either one. They were saying they could take care of (fix) your debt through consolidation. Personally, I did not want to go the route of debt consolidation. I felt I would have a better chance doing this on my own. I already had a budget and strong determination. With my continuous financial education, I felt very confident that I could do this. Also, no one knew my poor spending habits better than I did. Remember, your debt problems can be taken care of very easily—the biggest problem is your poor spending habits. Now, let's start on that debt.

It sounds so simple that it can't be true, but it is true. The first thing to do is to check with your money lenders to be sure there are no penalties for paying more than minimum payments. Also, check to be sure there are no penalties for early payoff. I have never had a problem with that; they were always just happy to get their money back. Then I started with the smallest debt first. Here is an easy example. Imagine you have four debts other than your house payment or rent.

1. Your car payoff is $12,000.
2. Your highest credit card debt is $8,000.
3. Your second credit card debt is $4,000.
4. Your third credit card debt is $3,000.

Continue to pay all your monthly payments on time (the key word here is *on time*). Now, think about how much money you have since you have stopped buying coffee on the way to work and stopped buying junk you do not need. That will add up fast. Remember how quickly you saved that emergency cash? Getting out of credit card debt will happen much quicker than you think. Now that your spending habits are under control, use that extra money to pay off the smallest debt first (in addition to the regular monthly payments on all your debts). In the example above, it would be the $3,000 debt. Hopefully, in just a few short months, that credit card debt will be gone.

After the $3,000 credit card debt is paid off, you now have the extra money from your good spending habits plus the regular monthly payment on the $4,000 card plus the regular monthly payment from the $3,000 debt—**all going toward paying off the $4,000 debt!** Now the real excitement starts! After the $4,000 debt falls in battle, the next debt ($8,000) will be assaulted by the regular monthly payment for the $8,000 debt plus the regular monthly payments formerly earmarked for your first two credit card victories and your good spending habits. Even though this debt is much larger than the other two that have already fallen, this one will still go fast because you can make larger payments now that the other two debts are history.

I guess you can see how quickly you will have the money to pay off the $12,000 loan. It happens so fast, and it is a great feeling. If you would like your debt reduction to happen even faster, I have a suggestion that worked well for me. Look around your house or apartment. I'm sure there are many things that you would not miss if you sold them. You may have a few hundred dollars'—maybe even a few thousand dollars'—worth of stuff! These might be things you have forgotten you even own. This is stuff that has no use or sentimental value to you or your family. Sell that stuff, and use all that extra money for your own personal debt-reduction battle.

Recently I was talking with someone who has a huge debt problem. I told him that I jump-started my debt reduction by selling something and putting that money toward debt reduction. I went on to tell him I sold something for $1,400 that had no use or sentimental value to me or my wife. He told me that sounded like a great idea and that his wife had some jewelry that she was planning on selling. Two weeks later he approached me with a huge smile on his face. He told me they sold that jewelry and received a little over $300 in exchange. I was very happy for him, at first. This could have been their start to debt reduction. But then, with that huge smile still on his face, he proceeded to tell me his wife bought more new shoes and also found a necklace that she didn't know she wanted until she saw it and felt she must own it. He bought a football jersey and sports memorabilia. They had forty dollars left over, so they had a big lunch and celebrated the new stuff they just bought. They did nothing toward their debt reduction; all they did was exchange stuff for stuff. Their debt problem is a result of their spending problem. They are not controlling their impulse buying.

As I'm rereading this chapter I thought this would be a good place for a proverb of Solomon. After all, I think no one can dispute his financial wealth. "The rich rule over the poor, and the borrower is servant to the lender" (Proverbs 22:7, NIV).

In my opinion debt reduction is similar to goal setting. If you set your goals too high, they will not be reached, and you will soon give up. You are setting yourself up for failure if you set your goals too high. Don't you think it is easier to pay off a $3000 loan than it is to pay off a $12,000 loan? Goals and budgets are always changing. Don't give up. Just change or modify your goals and budget. The important part is, "Don't give up! Stay focused and determined!" I know you can do it. All it takes is determination and a little time, but you can do it. Remember, poor spending habits were the beginning of all this debt to begin with.

A few days ago, I was on my way to meet a friend for lunch. On the way I was thinking about a particular golf club I was looking for. I realized I was going to pass by a second-hand store. I decided to stop in and look to see if they had this golf club. It was a long shot, (pardon the pun—I had to say it) and just as I thought, they didn't have it. On my way out, I could not help but notice a wall full of stuff. These shelves seemed to have everything. Plastic dolls, toaster ovens, spatulas, waffle irons, napkin holders, candle holders, cookie jars, small lamps—there was enough stuff there to fill a house! Please don't get me wrong. There is nothing wrong with any of these items if you need them. I observed people picking up each item, looking at it, then putting it back on the shelf. They were going from item to item with no expression on their faces. They looked as if they were in a hypnotic trance, maybe a magical shopping spell. *Pick up a coffee cup, look at it, put it back on the self, pick up a little toy, look at it, put it back on the shelf* with no expression on their faces, just a blank stare. My advice to you is to stop the mindless spending, and get out of debt. If you need something, buy it. If you don't need it, just walk out the same door you came in through. If you are buying too much useless stuff online, stop going online. You will feel better in the long run. Only you can take care of your poor spending habits, and only you can take care of your debt problem.

Remember that debt is an easy trap to fall into. It is not necessarily hard to get out of. It just takes determination and a little time. You can do it. My problem was just me and my buying, buying, and buying! Buying cars I did not need, buying motorcycles I did not need, (which caused more debt because of medical bills), buying so much stuff I did not need. I don't know if it was wisdom, maturity, or just being tired of not having money that caused me to have stress to the max. My seventeen-year-old truck is now a great encouragement to me. The old truck runs good. It just has a few small problems that could be fixed at very little cost, and I choose not to fix them. The air conditioning does not work, the radio does not work, and the inside door handle is broken. I have to put the window down and use the outside door handle to let myself out of the truck. I must look ridiculous letting myself out of a seventeen-year-old truck this way, but this is my encouragement, and it is a strong reminder of my past. It reminds me of how a vehicle used to be tied to my ego and self-esteem.

Yesterday I was sitting at a stoplight in my old beat-up truck, and I noticed a nice-looking, customized truck going through the intersection. I must have looked like a tired Labrador retriever, mouth wide open and tongue hanging out. Being the car enthusiast I am, I think only a couple drops of drool fell to my chin. Remember, debt reduction does take discipline. Whether you are a car enthusiast or boat enthusiast, or you enjoy shopping for new furniture every year. Or maybe you have an obsession with buying clothes or shoes. Remember that the first step to debt reduction is controlling your spending habits. I'm living proof that spending habits can be changed over time. Remember that customized truck I mentioned? One day soon I hope to have one, and if that happens, it will be paid for in full—no debt. I encourage you to look at your spending habits and get out of debt *as soon as possible.* You will feel so great when you are no longer paying those monthly car payments and credit card bills that seem to show up at the beginning of every month. Remember, if I can do it, I know you can do it

In Summary

1. Continue paying all bills on time.

2. Money saved by wiser spending habits plus the regular $3,000 loan payment go toward the $3,000 loan until the $3,000 loan is paid in full.

3. Money saved by wiser spending habits plus money formerly going toward the $3,000 loan and the regular

$4,000 loan payment all go toward the $4,000 loan until the $4,000 loan is paid in full.

4. Money saved by wiser spending habits plus money formerly going toward the $3,000 loan plus money formerly going toward the $4,000 loan and the regular $8,000 loan payment all go toward the $8,000 loan until the $8,000 loan is paid in full.

5. Money saved by wiser spending habits plus money formerly going toward the $3,000 loan plus money formerly going toward the $4,000 loan plus money formerly going toward the $8,000 loan and the regular $12,000 loan payment all go toward the $12,000 loan until that final loan is paid in full.

Chapter 9

Remaining Debt Free

Remaining debt free is a bit more challenging than I first thought. I assumed that after I was debt free, my battle with debt would be over. Your battle with debt may be over, but your temptation to purchase things will remain. This is a habit you developed during those instant-gratification days. Willpower, focused determination, and new good habits will cause these temptations to fade. Spending beyond your means will always be a temptation because it is a bad habit you have had for years. It is a temptation you must fight every day, but it will get much easier as time goes on. I suppose I could compare my bad spending habits to my bad smoking habit. After thirty years of smoking cigarettes, I finally quit. I no longer smoke cigarettes, although I still must fight the temptation of smoking. When I first quit smoking, I thought about having a cigarette every day, probably every hour or more. As time goes on, I think about it less and less.

Now I only think about it once or twice a year and that thought leaves my head in less than a minute.

Spending temptations are always present, even after you have stopped mindless spending in retail stores. They are still there after you have stopped that habit-forming online shopping, even if you have stopped giving much thought to those commercials on TV. You can still get tempted through the mail system. I got one a few days ago, and when I opened the envelope, in big bold letters it read, "FAST & AFFORDABLE". Still in big bold letters it continued on to read "LOAN AMOUNT $4,250, ARP 29.99% (36) MONTHLY PAYMENTS $180.39 / MO". If you were to borrow that money, statistics prove that most people would not pay that loan off early, and most people would use the full thirty-six months. OK, let's do the math:

$$\$180.39 \times 36 = \$6,494.04$$
(plus three more years of depressing debt)

That $4,250 loan costs you an additional $2,244.04! Come on people. Wake up and smell the coffee! Remaining debt free can be a bit challenging at first, but over time you will soon discover ads like this are no longer tempting. Actually they are almost comical. Later that same day, I was checking the voice mail on our home phone and there was a message. A stern authoritative voice said, "This is your last and final notice to lower your credit card interest rates." I don't even have a credit card anymore. I paid them all off. Like I said before, it's comical!

Remember in an earlier chapter when I mentioned we were upside down, or underwater (whichever term you would rather use), to the tune of about $45,000 on our house? One day I was going into the bank to make a deposit. Just as I walked in, a loan officer I had never seen before asked me if I would like to refinance my home. I told him we were too far upside down to get it refinanced. He reassured me he could get it refinanced with a lower interest rate through their bank. I knew he would be unable to refinance my home, but I thought, "Let's see what he can do." I was right; he could not refinance my home. Then he proceeded to tell me about all the different loans he could give me, like a car loan, home-improvement loan, and cash-advance loan. I told him I was not interested in a car loan. I told him I was completely debt free except for my home mortgage. For the next five minutes, he told me how stressed he was about having so many credit card payments plus a big car payment. My only thought was, "He's a loan officer. He should be able to see the trap he's falling into and the danger of borrowing money for liabilities" (you know, things that go down in value).

As I was leaving the bank, getting into my old truck, I was thinking how easy and so very tempting it was that with just a twist of a pen, the signing of a few papers, I could be driving the new car of my choice! Maybe I could buy a performance car or a classic car or quite possibly a high-end sports car. I made myself fight that feeling and did not give into the temptation. I reminded myself to stay the course of being debt free and remaining debt free. Remaining debt free was somewhat difficult for me, similar to when I quit smoking cigarettes. It was very difficult at first but got easier as time went by.

It's the same with your poor spending habits, it gets easier as time goes by, and hopefully with time the word *loan* will no longer be in your vocabulary. Fifteen years ago my hobby was race cars, which is a very expensive hobby. I remember one day I was talking with someone I knew, and the only thing we had in common was race cars. After we had talked about cars for about fifteen to twenty minutes, he went on to tell me his wife was going to be mad at him because he took out a loan against his home and was going to use that money to do some more major modifications to his race car. It's unbelievable how people get so obsessed with hobbies. I'm so glad I never crossed over that bridge. Remember, you cannot change your past. Yesterday is yesterday. Leave it, learn from it, and move on with your life! You cannot change your past; you can do something about your future.

I'm living proof that you can choose what path to take. Here is a perfect example of something that happened to me about a month ago. I told my wife I was going to buy a new set of golf clubs and new golf bag. My golf bag was in terrible shape, although the golf clubs would still do the job just fine. The problem was that I was missing two clubs I desperately needed for a good round of golf. If you are a golfer, this will make perfect sense. If you are not a golfer, you will still understand. I already had long irons and short irons. I was missing all my middle irons and my fairway woods. They were missing due to my bad temper. When I was younger, I managed to destroy all of them. I now have my temper under control due to many very positive changes in my life. I have also learned that the real game of golf is similar to life: you make a mistake, learn from it, and move on. It's a game of recovery. So the point is that I could get by just fine with a new five-iron, a new number three-fairway wood, my old clubs, and a new bag. But wouldn't a new shiny set of golf clubs be fun?

On my third time of going in this particular store that sells nothing but golf clubs and golf equipment, I had narrowed down my choices to a decision between two different sets of irons. As I was walking back and forth, comparing the two sets of irons, trying to decide which set to get, I was passing by the fairway woods

(I needed one of those also). The fairway wood that I wanted cost $185. Right beside that club was another club of the same brand. I asked the salesperson about the club. He said it was last year's model, and it was used, not new. It looked to be in good shape with very little use. I asked him the price of the used club. He said, "Twenty dollars"! At that very moment, I had made up my mind. I was only going to buy two clubs and one bag. I gave the man a twenty-dollar bill and walked out of the store.

Three days later my wife and I were out for a round of golf. In the golf course clubhouse there was a golf bag packed full of clubs of different brands and different types with a sign that read, "Fifteen dollars per club."

As I was looking at golf bags, my wife approached me and asked, "Honey, is this the golf club you have been looking for?"

I said, "It sure is. Where did you find it?"

She told me she had gotten it out of the bag in the corner, and it was only $15. (She is such a great shopper!) They also had used golf bags that were in excellent shape for $50. That is close to one-fourth the price of a new bag! My total cost was only $85 dollars for those three items that I actually needed. If I had bought a full set of everything new, it was going to be a little over $1,000!

The irony of that story is that when I had no money and poor spending habits, I would have used a credit card and bought all new stuff. Now that I have the money to buy all new stuff, I decided to buy three used items that were great brands and in great shape. Poor spending habits coupled with foolish, meaning-less priorities can be changed. If you choose to become debt free and remain debt free, you can do it! Simply choose the path you need to take. What happened in the past happened in the past. Your financial future is yours, so take charge of it now. Just like in the game of golf, "recovery" starts from where you are today.

Chapter 10

Having Fun on Less Money

Hopefully you will keep this in mind as you start your debt battle. Remember the spending cutbacks? You can do this with your entertainment money as well. Temporarily, you may need to stop going to expensive entertainment parks, weekend mountain hideaways, or island retreats. Doing things like this can get very expensive. I'm not saying never do these things again. All I'm saying is you should wait until your debt is paid off. Through good marketing and the use of the media, *they* have you totally convinced that if you don't spend a lot of money, you're not going to have a lot of fun. This may sound a little harsh and one-sided, but don't forget you are entering a debt **battle**. You must pick a side. Do you want to remain enslaved to debt or become debt free? Remember in an earlier chapter when I mentioned going to the park, a car show, the beach, or a lake for inexpensive entertainment? Here are a few more examples of what my wife and I did and still do today because they are fun.

These are things you can do if you are single, married, on a date, or with other friends. We happen to live near a large coastal, historical tourist town, and we both enjoy being a tourist in our own town. Finding a parking place downtown can be a big hassle. On the other side of the harbor (which is an easier drive for us plus free parking), there is a boat taxi, and a round trip ticket from that dock to the downtown dock is ten dollars per person. It's about a twenty minute boat ride each way. It's a very enjoyable boat ride, and about half the time, we see dolphins along the way. We spend most of the day looking at historical sites, and we might grab a hot dog from a vendor. If there is a group of us, we may stop for a light lunch (most restaurant lunch menus are much cheaper than dinner). This all day affair can be very inexpensive and a lot of fun.

How about this for another idea? Take some of the money you normally spend at the grocery store and go to a farmers' market for your fresh produce. Be careful. It is still very easy to overspend, so take a small amount of money, and when that money is gone, you're done. No more spending! This will help make you wise about your spending.

Tennis anyone (check with your doctor first)? If you live in an apartment complex, most of them have tennis courts. If you don't live in an apartment with tennis courts, or you live in a house, most counties have tennis courts where you can play. One time I lived in a county that had beautiful tennis courts. If my memory serves me correctly, I think it was five dollars to play all day (although the southern summer sun would normally last longer than I did).

Have you ever wanted to learn how to play golf? Maybe a good place to start would be with a friend that knows the game enough to teach you. The two of you could go to a driving range.

A good practice range has all the disciplines of the game, and it's only about ten dollars for a bucket of golf balls. Many of them also loan clubs for free or rent them for about $1 a piece. That's inexpensive for one to two hours of practice. You still need to have things to do in life that you enjoy. You do not want to sit at home having no fun, or you will be tempted to give up on the battle. Items that also provide fresh air and exercise give you the best of all worlds. It's a lot cheaper than a jumbo bucket of popcorn and a large soda at the movies!

Speaking of going to the movies, try going to the matinee—it's cheaper! About that huge bucket of popcorn and that overpriced candy, and don't forget about that extra-large soda you always get that is so big you need two hands just to carry it—moderation is the key. Decide what your favorite type of entertainment is, and find ways to make good financial and health choices for yourself and your family. There is nothing wrong with going to the movies or with eating popcorn, candy, or soda occasionally. Too much of this type of good thing can affect your overall health as well as your financial health.

As you read this, you probably realize that I'm a doer and not a watcher. If you do not like the things I just mentioned, or maybe you are looking for something that is a little less strenuous, try checking in your town or a town nearby for a "meet the local artist" event. They are usually free or close to free. My wife and I went to one that was huge and free. They had artwork inside and local musicians outside. We spent the better part of the day there. We had a great time, and the only money we spent was on a ten-dollar CD from a local musician and a three-dollar bag of kettle corn from a local vendor. We had a great time and only spent thirteen dollars. I'm sure you can think of some things you would really enjoy doing that cost little money.

This may be a perfect time to invite a close friend or family member over and discuss the debt battle you are preparing for. Who knows, maybe they will want to start their own debt battle? Looking back, maybe I should have told a friend or family member what I was doing about my decision to wage war against debt, but I did not. I kept it to myself. If I were to give advice on this, it would be to find a close friend you can trust. You can discuss this book and discuss your plan for your debt battle.

Remember, when cutting back on wasteful spending, be sure to find fun things to do using less money, or you may be tempted to quit. If you have an expensive hobby, maybe you need to put that on hold temporarily. You can always go back to that expensive hobby after you become debt free. You can slowly work money back into the budget for that later. You may realize later that you don't like that hobby as much, after you realize how much money it was costing you. After becoming debt free, you're going to start looking at money and hobbies much differently.

I don't understand why some people will spend one or more hours a day studying sports statistics, reading celebrity news, or studying and researching wine or any other personal interest and then absolutely refuse to study their own finances. I'm sorry if this seems harsh, but this really hits home to me. I am in my fifties and wasted so many opportunities that I hope you will be wise enough not to waste. I hope that you will start working on your own finances and educate yourself for your own financial success.

Chapter 11

Focusing on the Future

From time to time I look back at my past, at things I've done right and things I've done wrong. I reflect on my past, although I do not dwell on it. I look toward the future with a positive attitude and a large dose of reality check. It's because of that reality check that we decided to open a second emergency fund. This emergency fund is a completely separate checking account and, once again, is for emergencies only. If we both went jobless and had zero income, we could survive for over six months on this money without touching any of our 401(k) money or investment money. We have also decided to start setting money aside to acquire assets.

Webster's Dictionary defines **assets**:
1. **Anything owned that has exchange value**
2. **A valuable or desirable thing to have**

Just like the definition for liabilities in chapter 1 of this book, *Webster's* goes on to further define the word assets by using it as an accounting term.

3. *Accounting*: **all the entries on a balance sheet showing the entire resources of a person or business, tangible and intangible, as accounts and notes receivable, cash, inventory, equipment, real estate, good will, etc.**

All my life I have been very good at buying liabilities—you know, things that go down in value, like cars, trucks, motorcycles, and the list goes on. Since my wife and I are both focused on acquiring assets for our future, we do not want to forget about or neglect paying our mortgage on time. The key word here is **on time**. Check with your mortgage lender to be sure that if you pay extra money, it goes toward principal without penalties. What I'm doing is paying double principal (not double payments). Example: let's say your house payment is $1,421 a month, and the principal this month is only $205. Let's assume you are paying $785 in interest and $431 into escrow. My suggestion would be to pay a minimum of $205 extra on your mortgage. That would be a payment of $1626 in this example. This is a big loan, and it will take some time to pay it off. Just remember, it is not hard to make larger payments when you no longer have those monthly credit card payments as well as that monthly car payment.

As I mentioned before, we are also setting money aside for acquiring assets. Our assets will become passive income for our future.

Here are a couple examples of what is meant by passive income:

- A business that is owned and the owner of the business does not need to be present every day for the business to be profitable.

- Real estate that produces a positive cash flow through rent.

My wife and I are very excited about our future together, both spiritually as well as financially. We are very positive about our future, and we look forward to next week, next month, and next year. Believe me it's easier to stay positive when you do not have credit card bills and car payments hanging over your head. I feel the three biggest downers as well as the three easiest traps to fall into are the following:

1. Credit card or car payment debt
2. Mindless TV
3. Negative people

I hate to be around negative people. These are the people who are usually unhappy, usually complaining, and will quickly shoot down any positive idea you or someone else may have. No matter what you say, they complain. They complain about their jobs, the price of gas, real estate prices, and politics. I frequently hear most people complaining about the weather. It's too hot or it's too cold, there's too much rain or not enough rain—complaining, complaining, so much complaining. Although after a huge hurricane, I was without electricity for almost a month, with very little food or water, and I may have complained a little bit! Why should people complain about things they have no control over. All of our close friends are very positive people, and in my opinion there is a big difference between a positive person that is just having a bad day and a negative person. Remember, if you spend most of your time complaining, this only clouds your thoughts with negativity and leaves you with less time for creative thinking. In fact, negativity actually stifles creativity! It's a big waste of time and energy, and we try to avoid these people altogether.

I said that there were three easy traps to fall into, actually there is a fourth. Procrastination is a thief of time. Please do not procrastinate after you finish reading this book. Start immediately on your plan to reduce your debt. Not long ago I was speaking with someone about debt reduction. He asked me if I could make a suggestion. I recommended a book he could buy. A week later I ask him if he had finished reading the book. He said he had only finished one chapter. Two weeks later I asked him if he had finished the book. He told me he had been busy. On the third week, I asked him if he had finished the book, and he told me he was busy. I asked him if he had been working a lot of overtime. He said no. He had been watching sports on TV and playing video games. Six months later I saw him and we started to talk about debt. His debt problem had increased. Although he could tell me a lot of sports facts, and he mentioned he was getting quite good at video games. If he does not change soon, he will remain in debt for the rest of his life.

If you procrastinate, there is a strong possibility you will never start, and you may remain in debt for the rest of your life. Start on your debt reduction battle now. Do not wait for next month or next year. Do it now. I realized that I got myself into debt, so I got myself out of debt. Remember, I'm not a financial expert. I'm just an average guy with a lot of determination.

A couple of days ago, I went to the mall. Don't laugh, it happens. There's a large bookstore there. Before I went into the bookstore to get another financial book, I decided to grab a bite to eat at a fast-food restaurant in the mall. As I was eating my sandwich and sipping on a cup of coffee, I noticed an older lady with a severe limp. She was cleaning tables. She looked as though she was in her late sixties or early seventies. My heart was broken when I saw her struggling to walk while going from table to table wiping them off. Forty years ago, she probably did not imagine herself working in a noisy mall with not enough money saved for retirement. With the rising cost of living, she must feel trapped. "But wait," you may say, "maybe she likes to work." If this is the case, don't you think she would rather be volunteering at a charitable organization that she believes in? Possibly her lifelong passion has been bird watching or collecting seashells on a secluded beach with only the sounds of the waves crashing on shore and the seagulls flying overhead! Her goal was probably not cleaning tables in a noisy mall. As I got up to take my trash and tray to its proper location, I made a special point to walk past her, and I said, "You have a wonderful day, ma'am." I was hoping to see a true genuine smile. She politely smiled back and said, "Thank you, sir," but I could still see the sadness in her eyes. She has been such an inspiration to me! She has made me realize how much I want you and all of your family to have the information you need to make sound financial choices.

You are the reason for this book. You, the lady in the mall, my friends from work, the folks that have asked me about financial information, the young people starting out, the people hoping to retire "someday"—all of you! Remember, time is like a thief in the night: it sneaks up on you very fast, and you are unaware it is happening until it's too late. The way to be ready for the future is to take care of your debt today.

Chapter 12

Final Thoughts

Getting out of credit card debt is something you really need to do. For me, getting out of credit card debt started with my desire to be free from the debt burden and reading an inspirational financial book my wife bought me. Since then my financial book collection has blossomed to over sixty books. The subjects of these books include real estate, stocks, debt reduction, and business. I wanted to know how money really works, and I still do want to learn as much as I can to stay ahead. Acquiring knowledge through financial books can be a very powerful tool for your tool belt. This tool is not only for today's debt but also for tomorrow's financial success. I want to be the captain of my financial ship, not merely a passenger, because up to now all the finance companies and banks were the captains. I was just a passenger on a rough ride, and believe me, it was quite a ride—a ride that I do not want to take again.

I encourage you to stop watching boring mindless TV and start reading financial books. If you don't like to read all the time, that's OK. Neither do I. That's why more than half my financial books are audiobooks, and there are some really good ones out there. I seem to get the most out of them when I treat them like a seminar without any outside distractions. I do not listen to them while I am working out at the gym, driving a car, or talking on the phone. I concentrate on what I'm hearing only. I try to give it my full attention just like I would an excellent seminar.

Have you ever been to a really good seminar, and about half-way through you say to yourself, "I sure wish I was taking notes"? Or halfway through you realize you were taking so many notes that you may have missed the big picture? This is the great thing about audiobooks. You can always stop it, back it up, and listen to it again. Sometimes, I enjoy listening to an audiobook I have not listened to for about six months. Almost every time, I catch something that I missed the first time, or maybe it is through continuous education that I finally understand. I'm not sure, but it works for me.

I encourage you to go to the bookstore or go online and look in the financial section for either paper or audiobooks on debt reduction. This is a great place to start. A few years ago, I realized I needed to be on the success curve financially, and this is only possible through knowledge and action.

I enjoy these audiobooks so much that once a week a friend of mine comes over and we eat pizza or have sandwiches and snacks while we listen to an audiobook for about one to two hours. I think eventually this number will climb to about four or five people. We discuss debt reduction and acquiring assets for future passive income. Looking back, this all started with my wife buying me one financial book and my own determination to succeed.

I feel that setting goals for your financial freedom is a crucial part of this battle. I also like to set personal goals. I think it can be fun. When I do this, I try to be realistic. There is a big difference between goals and pipe dreams. Pipe dreams are fantasies about your future that bounce around in your head for five minutes and then they are gone. They don't have a real plan on how to make them reality. Both personal goals and financial goals need to be well thought out and well planned. When you are putting together your financial plan (goals), try to be realistic with your numbers. Make them goals that are obtainable with proper planning, a lot of determination, and some spending changes. After reading this book, try setting goals for yourself. You can do this. Imagine how you will feel when you become debt free!

Whenever I'm speaking with someone about debt reduction, more often than not, they ask me if there is a single book I can recommend. I always say that I gain knowledge out of all of them. Some are more conservative financially than others, but they all have useful points. It is up to you to decide your financial plan after consulting multiple sources. I must say I really enjoy listening to audiobooks that are inspirational. I have many of those as well. That being said, here are twelve books that I highly recommend. These twelve books should help get you going in the right direction. These books are available in audiobook form if you would rather just listen. Just think, there is one for each month! In only one year, think of the wealth of knowledge you can acquire! This could be one of your yearly goals. I have listed them alphabetically by author.

- *Start Over, Finish Rich* by David Bach, published by Random House, Inc.

- *The 7 Habits of Highly Effective People* by Stephen R. Covey, published by Franklin Covey Co.

- *The Compound Effect* by Darren Hardy, published by Success Books

- *Rich Dad, Poor Dad* by Robert T. Kiyosaki and Sharon L. Lechter, C.P.A., published by Business Plus

- *Increase Your Financial IQ* by Robert T Kiyosaki, published by Hachette Audio

- *Put Your Dreams to the Test* by John C. Maxwell, published by Thomas Nelson, Inc.

- *Sometimes You Win Sometimes You Learn* by John C. Maxwell, published by Hachette Audio

- *The Slight Edge* by Jeff Olson, published by Success Books

- *The Total Money Makeover* by Dave Ramsey, published by Thomas Nelson, Inc.

- *The Millionaire Next Door* by Thomas J. Stanley, PhD, and William D. Danko, PhD, published by Simon & Schuster, Inc.

- *The Millionaire Mind* by Thomas J. Stanley, PhD, published by Simon & Schuster, Inc.

- *See You at the Top* by Zig Ziglar, published by Nightingale-Conant Corporation

There is also another book I recommend. It's not a book you would find in the financial section of a bookstore. It's a book about life; the fears we all have; and how we can replace fear with peace, hope, and faith. The name of this book is *Fearless* by Max Lucado. We own the hard-cover book and the audiobook. Like I said before, I enjoy audiobooks. I even have the Bible in audiobook form as well as in the traditional-looking, soft-bonded black leather with ultrathin pages and about two inches of a silk bookmark hanging out of the bottom. Sometimes I read, but most of the time I enjoy just sitting back and listening.

Recently, I was riding in a car with a friend of mine who I will call my financial mentor. We were on the way to look at some property he recently purchased. We were talking about property, financial seminars, and money in general. About halfway to the destination, he asked me if I had a garage so I could start working (playing) with old classic cars again. I proceeded to tell him that I had sworn off expensive liabilities until I learned how to acquire assets and started to gain wealth through passive income. I must have talked for about five to ten minutes about *no more debt* and *no more liabilities*. As we slowed down for a stoplight, I must have run out of breath and stopped talking. He quietly asked me if I had ever thought about public speaking on debt reduction. I said, "No, why do you ask?" He looked me straight in the eye and told me that it was because I spoke from the heart.

I am speaking from the heart in this book, too. I have come through many difficulties in my life. Many of them could have been avoided with some sound financial planning. It is my hope that this book will help you avoid the mistakes I have made.

I'm sure you've heard the expression that you learn from your own mistakes. That is true, and it can help keep you from repeating them. It is often easier to learn from other people's mistakes, but you can also learn from other people's successes. This is why I encourage you to read financial books as well as financial success stories. They're very inspirational. I highly recommend that you make it a daily habit to study finances. Read financial books as well as financial success stories every day. Also, you may want to listen to an inspirational audiobook. If you start to feel overwhelmed, this can be a big help. Stay focused on your debt reduction. Now is not the time to give up.

Try to make it a habit to turn off the TV and turn on the mind. You may even become bored or "turned off" by TV. One day you may realize how much time you're wasting watching those boring, mind-numbing sitcoms or watching that extremely depressing the-world-is-falling-apart news. (Let's not forget about all those commercials that are trying to keep you enslaved to material things.) Very soon you will discover the true satisfaction of working on your own finances as well as studying financially successful people and how they gained their wealth through knowledge, action, honesty, and integrity. For me this seems to be a better use of time. It's more stimulating for my mind and better for my soul. It works for me. Give it a try. I don't think you will be disappointed.

As you read the success stories, you will realize these people have one thing in common: they all stay focused, stay determined, and use a lot of creativity. I admire them. I get so inspired and get so much out of reading their books or listening to their stories, and I hope you do the same. Remember that *you* got yourself in debt, and only *you* can get yourself out of debt. I'm sure you must feel sometimes that life has put you in a boat that is dragging a heavy anchor. Life didn't do that to you—being enslaved to the credit card did. Pull up the anchor and reset your course, start from where you are now so you can have a debt-free life. Remember to stay focused and determined.

In closing I suppose I should say something like, "Good luck." I'm not going to say that, because luck has nothing to do with it. Change will only happen when you make the commitment to become debt free. I truly hope this book has inspired you to start working on your debt problem and that my book recommendations will help with your future financial success. I truly hope you have enjoyed reading this book as much as I have enjoyed writing it. So in closing, "Good luck!" Oops, I said it.